FAMILY,
GOVERNMENT,
AND CHURCH

FAMILY, GOVERNMENT, AND CHURCH

Relating Three Jurisdictions of
Divinely Delegated Authority

BRET LAIRD

We have often heard that Scripture commands us to submit to government unless it demands us to go against God. In times past, there has been great need to emphasize the need for submission. In present days, the church must carefully discern the precise line where government compels us to go against God. We should be thankful that brothers and sisters in the persecuted church have spent much time contemplating these very issues.

This work reflects a helpful distillation of these insights. While affirming the need to honor those over us, Laird helps us to think through how Scripture, as the ultimate authority, establishes divinely delegated authority within the family, church, and the government. These truths inform our conscience and connect with other biblical passages that factor into our response to government. Balancing all of that demands wisdom.

Drawing upon his missionary experience, Laird practically helps us to see how to think through the whole counsel of God in evaluating a situation. Do not let the concise nature of this work deceive you. Each part of it is filled with thought-provoking insights. As you grapple with them, they will help you be better equipped to know how to respond in a fully biblical way to our ever-changing times.

ABNER CHOU, PH.D.: Interim President and John F. MacArthur Endowed Fellow, The Master's University

Family, Government, and Church is both clear and thorough. It is not only intensely scriptural, but it also answers the unexpressed questions and tensions of the heart. I am not aware of a modern-day resource that speaks to this issue as robustly and carefully as this one. Bret Laird has served us well.

DR. JAMES COATES: Pastor-Teacher, GraceLife Church, Edmonton, Alberta, Canada

My great-grandfather was shot for his faith, and both of my grandfathers suffered much for Christ during the Soviet era. However, I never heard in their words or prayers hatred and unforgiveness toward their persecutors. Nor did they ever deny the need for government authority. I saw their trust in God and obedience to His plan. At the same time, they had a lot of unique wisdom on how to remain faithful to God in the face of a godless government, while building up the church, taking care of the family, and not losing their human dignity as bearers of the image of God. In many ways, my training in pastoral ministry began by observing my grandfathers' lives.

Brother Bret's successful ministry in the former Soviet Union allowed him to form a more holistic concept of the Christian view of the state, church, and family. His excellent understanding of contemporary American culture and accurate exegesis of the biblical texts helped him to write a practical book that gives clear principles for guidance and sound decision-making in these now controversial areas. Since the book is full of pastoral wisdom and care, it can safely be used for small groups or individual reading. It would even make a good gift for your local politicians and public servants!

EVGENY BAKHMUTSKY: Pastor-teacher of the Russian Bible Church Baptist (Moscow), Doctor of Practical Theology

What a timely book! In a world that wants to redefine terms and redirect our attention and our allegiance, Pastor Bret Laird reminds us to go back to the Bible. The book recognizes that while God is sovereign over human affairs, He also set limits to governments. Because of the sinful human condition, human governments have abused their God-given power over millennia. There is a time to submit to obey and there is a time to resist the government that demands worship or prevents worship. The book has great insights and helps the believer discern when the government has overstepped its authority and how the believer should respond. May we heed the words of Jesus to be "shrewd as serpents and innocent as doves" (Matthew 10:16).

TIBERIUS RATA, PH.D.: Professor of Old Testament Studies; Associate Dean; Grace College and Theological Seminary, Winona Lake, Indiana

In his brief book, the author raises relevant and just questions regarding the established human authorities. His integral approach of ascending through the "theological pyramid" enables the book to escape superficiality, enables the reader to observe the process of a deep study of key biblical texts, and to glean specific principles to apply in life.

I am a pastor in a country in the 10/40 window, where more than 99 percent of the population is Muslim. Christians in my country constantly encounter pressure and persecution not only from their families and the society, but also from governmental authorities. In theory, our nation upholds full freedom of religion, but the reality is far different. Laws are passed which have an extremely restrictive character, which create burdensome registration requirements, forbid proselytism, and require official permission from religious organizations to communicate with fellow believers abroad. The participation of children under the age of eighteen in religious gatherings is forbidden. It is not rare for government agents to resort to intimidation, humiliation, threats, and insults to incentivize people to become informants, and to impose heavy fines. While experiencing life in this context firsthand, questions arise as to how to respond in this or that situation, and how to relate to governmental authority. The systematic presentation and drawing of clear boundaries between the three institutions of authority helped me to organize my existing knowledge and to see the purpose and responsibility of each. The author, using the analogy of a traffic light, helps the reader to see the principles of red-, green-, and yellow-light issues, and that none of the institutions of power should invade the exclusive area of another, in order to avoid a catastrophic result.

Bret is not one-sided in application. He is the pastor of a large American church, but his many years of ministry experience in post-Soviet countries enables him to consider some practical aspects from different perspectives. The book will be helpful for Christians in different parts of the world, because it is founded not on personal or cultural biases, but on the Word of God.

NAME WITHHELD: (For security reasons)

Family, Government, and Church will be a blessing to every Christian, Christian family, and person seeking truth. The author's careful exegesis of the Word of God, and fifteen years as a missionary professor in former communist countries, present many compelling insights. Persecuted pastors and church members found the Bible sufficient for strength and hope, and to guide them victoriously through challenging experiences.

DR. BOB PROVOST: President Emeritus, the Slavic Gospel Association

In the last couple of years, Christians in USA entered into a previously unknown—to the territory of conflicts between their convictions and demands of the government. From everything that we can see, the number of these situations will only grow. To have clear and strong convictions in such circumstances is an absolute necessity for every believer. Without them, we will be easily overrun by outside pressure. Bret Laird's book is an excellent resource, helping to form such convictions. Deep exposition of key Bible passages and clear application of them in different life scenarios make this book convincing and practical.

ALEXEY KOLOMIYTSEV: Pastor, Word of Grace Bible Church, www.slovo.org

Family, Government, and Church
Relating Three Jurisdictions of Divinely
Delegated Authority
Bret Laird

Copyright © 2021 Shepherd Press

ISBNS:
Paper: 978-1-63342-246-9
ePub: 978-1-63342-247-6
Mobi: 978-1-63342-248-3

Cover design and typeset by www.greatwriting.org

Printed in the United States of America

Shepherd Press
P.O. Box 24
Wapwallopen, PA 18660
www.shepherdpress.com

This book is co-branded with TMAI. All royalties from the sale
of this book will be donated to TMAI to help provide biblical
resources for pastoral training centers around the world.
www.tmai.org

Contents

This book is dedicated to my brothers and sisters in Christ around the world who are being persecuted for giving Christ "first place in everything" (Colossians 1:18).

I have tried to write with paper and ink the lessons you have taught us with blood and bars.

It has been a great privilege to know some of you. It will be a great honor to meet all of you when Christ has crowned your suffering with glory.

"Stand firm in your faith, knowing that the same experiences of suffering are being experienced by your brethren throughout the world. After you have suffered for a little while, the God of all grace, who called you to His eternal glory in Christ, will Himself perfect, confirm, strengthen and establish you. To Him be dominion forever and ever. Amen."

1 Peter 5:9–11

Foreword

We are witnessing in our generation the greatest threats to the authority of the church, not only in America but around the world. Globalization has enabled a universal adoption of a progressive worldview, which is counterbiblical, as well as the activation of a universal government response to events such as the COVID pandemic. Many pastors are facing direct threats, government intrusion, and restrictions not only related to gathering for worship, but accusations and regulation on what is believed and taught.

For many pastors and congregations, intolerance by cultural elites has turned to political activism, which goes against long-held freedoms protected by their country's constitutional laws. The need exists for a clear and accessible biblical treatment on the matter of authority. Without clarity and conviction on this subject, the church faces the internal threat of division over conflicting interpretations on the matter. Pastors and elders are being forced to look more carefully at what the Scriptures teach, enabling believers to develop discernment on this critical issue. Believers must understand which authorities have been ordained by God, and what duties and limitations these authorities possess.

Where there has been historic agreement between the laws of the land and the view of Scripture, the church has been able to hold to a simplistic interpretation of texts such as Romans 13. But when conflict emerges between the duty to God and duty to men, a simplistic view must yield to a more exegetically defined view of authority showing that all authorities are not equal or without limits. Today's realities present a set of increasing threats directed at the church, the family, and the individual. A more careful study of the realms of authority and how the believer best obeys God's call to honor and submit to authorities will serve the church, not only today, but in even more perilous times ahead.

It is important to note that we who are facing such threats can find encouragement not only from the Scriptures, but from the testimony of faithful Christians around the world who have without compromise faced persecution. From the early church, throughout the Reformation, and until today, the church has always faced assault from secular states. Where there has been persecution, pastors and church leaders have found their source of strength in the authority of God's Word, which is sufficient to equip God's people to think and act in accord with Christ's mind on the matter. Bret Laird knows this from his own personal ministry experience, serving in places where the church faithfully faced some of the cruelest attacks. His training of pastors who know firsthand the extremes government can go to, to subvert the voice of the church and the gospel message, informs and motivates his writing of this study.

What has occurred in other foreign nations is now recognizably seen increasing within Western countries. May the Lord use this timely book to aid His church to be faithful and unified as it faces the challenges of the day, and may it remind you that God is ultimately sovereign and will accomplish His good and His glory if we persevere in the face of danger.

MARK TATLOCK
President, The Masters Academy International

Introduction

Christians in America have enjoyed a level of religious freedom, safety, and societal acceptance unprecedented in church history. To have this much freedom for this long is a historical anomaly, and should be a cause of tremendous gratitude.

Because so many successive generations of believers have lived in a context where the state protects believers rather than persecutes them, the church in America has not needed to think very deeply about the extent and limits of the authority God has delegated to government. Most church members do not have even a basic understanding of related biblical teaching, and most pastors have sensed no compelling reason to devote preaching and teaching time to a topic that has seemed rather irrelevant to their flock.

But the socio-political context in which we live and minister is changing rapidly, and it is becoming increasingly important for believers and churches to develop a robust and biblical theology of government. Believers and churches may face some high-stakes choices in the near future, so we urgently need to equip them to understand and apply what God's Word teaches about the extent and limits of three key jurisdictions of divinely delegated authority: the *family*, the *government*, and the *church*.

In this brief introduction to a much larger topic, we will attempt to answer three basic questions:

1.   What should a believer's attitude and perspective be toward human government?
2.   How can we know when we are supposed to submit to government (Romans 13:1), and when we must "obey God rather than men" (Acts 5:29)?
3.   How can we know when the government authorities have exceeded the limits of their divinely ordained authority and intruded on authority which God has given exclusively to the church or to the family?

Since this book is the outcome of a three-part sermon series I preached in August-September 2020, my style will be exhortational, not academic, and I will focus primarily on the text on which those messages were based: Romans 12:14–13:7. So let's prayerfully and carefully study God's Word to find the answers to those three vital questions.

1

A Believer's Attitude and Perspective

What should a believer's attitude and perspective be toward human government?

....

Since human governments are so often inefficient, incompetent, and indifferent, it is tempting for us as believers to view them with disgust and contempt, even when we are *not* being persecuted or treated unjustly. But it is when persecution begins that the temptation to *hate* the government becomes especially intense.

Unlike our brothers and sisters in other parts of the world, American believers haven't had to watch bulldozers destroy their church building, see their pastor arrested in the middle of a service, watch children being taken away from their parents, or see fellow believers murdered in the streets. But in Romans 12:14–21, which is the preceding context for one of the most important passages on human government (Rom. 13:1–7), the apostle Paul is writing to believers who *had* seen and experienced such things.

Nero was the emperor, and he was a cruel, capricious persecutor of the church. If there was anyone who deserved to be hated and cursed, he was the one. But instead, Paul, alluding to the teaching of Jesus in the Sermon on the Mount, instructs the believers in Rome to:

> Bless those who persecute you; bless and do not curse. Rejoice with those who rejoice, and weep with those who weep. Be of the same mind toward one another; do not be haughty in mind, but associate with the lowly. Do not be wise in your own estimation. Never pay back evil for evil to anyone. Respect what is right in the sight of all men. If possible, so far as it depends on you, be at peace with all men. Never take your own revenge, beloved, but leave room for the wrath *of God,* for it is written, "VENGEANCE IS MINE, I WILL REPAY," SAYS THE LORD. "BUT IF YOUR ENEMY IS HUNGRY, FEED HIM, AND IF HE IS THIRSTY, GIVE HIM A DRINK; FOR IN SO DOING YOU WILL HEAP BURNING COALS ON HIS HEAD." Do not be overcome by evil, but overcome evil with good. (Romans 12:14–21)

I want to draw your attention to the personal nature of the language in verse 14: "Bless *those* who persecute you. . ." The call here is not to bless the government as an abstract entity, but to bless the *individuals* who were personally involved in ordering or carrying out the persecution.

We are often tempted to think of government as an amorphous *thing*—and it doesn't seem wrong to hate, mock, and seek vengeance against a *thing*—but we need to remember that *human governments* are made up of *human beings*. Just like us, they are people who are made in the image of God, have an eternal soul, and desperately need salvation.

In Titus 3:3, Paul tells Titus to remind believers that they have a lot in common with the governing officials who were persecuting them. He writes:

> Remind them to be subject to rulers, to authorities, to be obedient, to be ready for every good deed, to malign no one, to be peaceable, gentle, showing every consideration for all men. For we also once were foolish ourselves, disobedient, deceived, enslaved to various lusts and pleasures, spending our life in malice and envy, hateful, hating one another. But when the kindness of God our Savior and His love for mankind appeared, He saved us, not on the basis of deeds which we have done in righteousness, but according to His mercy, by the washing of regeneration and renewing by the Holy Spirit, whom He poured out upon us richly through Jesus Christ our Savior, so that being justified by His grace we would be made heirs according to the hope of eternal life. (Titus 3:1-7)

Believers need to remember that they, too, were once lost and at enmity with Christ. They need to remember that individual government officials—even those who are persecuting them—have an eternal soul and are just a heartbeat away from hell. So our attitude and perspective toward them should be one of compassion, not hatred; of evangelism, not revenge; of respect, not contempt; of love, not hatred.

We can hate and mock government officials, or we can pray for them and preach Christ to them—but we can't do both. The option that Scripture calls upon us to do is crystal clear:

> First of all, then, I urge that entreaties and prayers, petitions and thanksgivings, be made on behalf of all men, for kings and all who are in authority, so that we may lead a tranquil and quiet life in all godliness and dignity. This is good and acceptable in the sight of God our Savior, who desires all men to be saved and to come to the knowledge of the truth.
> (1 Timothy 2:1–4)

God desires them to be saved, and therefore that must be our desire as well. So regardless of how we might feel about them personally, and no matter how we feel about their policies and performance, government officials should be the subject of our prayers, not the object of our ridicule.

Christian, do not mock your mission field! The mayors, the governors, the congressmen, the judges, the president, and the rest of our government officials are eternal souls who need Christ. So we should be praying for them, not mocking them. It may well be that our elected officials and unelected bureaucrats often act in ways that are unjust, unrighteous, and unfitting for the importance and dignity of their office. But is it right to respond to their sin by committing the exact same type of sin ourselves?

As a believer, you hold an office, too. You are an *ambassador* of Christ. You are part of a *royal priesthood*. You are the representative of a righteous King and His eternal kingdom—so juvenile ridicule and heartless mockery are below the dignity and purpose of your office. You should not respond to politicians making a mockery of the office *they* hold by making a mockery of the office *you* hold. Keep in mind that you are an ambassador and a royal priest. So think, speak, and act like one!

It is true that opposing evil and advocating for righteousness is part of your role as salt and light in the world—but there is a right and a wrong way to do that! It is also true that the apostles and prophets sometimes used both open rebuke and pointed satire to expose the folly of sin and evil. But there is a distinct difference between polemical satire and personal slander. The Bible instructs believers to speak out against evil, but it also gives instructions regarding how to do so. Whether you are confronting evil and advocating for righteousness in a biblical or unbiblical way will be very evident in how you speak about government officials—especially at home and in the things you say on social media portals.

You should be sure you're viewing and treating government officials *as individuals who are created in the image of God and have an eternal soul.* As an ambassador of the gospel of Christ, you must heed the command of Romans 12:14b: "Bless and do not curse."

How should we view government?
Principle #1
We should view it as being made up of individuals with eternal souls (Romans 12:14–21).

With that important first point in mind, we now consider Romans 13, where we'll find the second way we should view government:

> Every person is to be in subjection to the governing authorities. For there is no authority except from God, and those which exist are established by God.
> (Romans 13:1)

Notice that the command to submit to governing authorities is given to "every person." No one is above the law, and everyone is commanded by God to "be in subjection to the governing authorities." In the American context, this means that each of us as an individual citizen is to submit to our local, state, and federal authorities.

But it also means that local, state, and federal officials themselves are not above the law. "*Every* person" is to submit. They, too, must "be in subjection to the governing authorities" above them. In the United States, the will of the people as expressed in fair and free elections is the ultimate civil authority. The constitution, not any government official or agency, is the highest law in the land. And there is a separation and balance of powers, both between the executive, legislative, and judicial branches, and between local, state, and federal governments.

So the command to "be in subjection to the governing authorities" applies to *every* citizen and to *every* government official. The Greek term translated "be in subjection" is *hupotasso*. It is a compound word, consisting of a preposition meaning "under" and a verb meaning "to rank." So it means to "rank yourself under" and was commonly used in military contexts to describe the duty a soldier has to submit to his superiors and follow their orders. So the command, as applied to citizens, is clear:

- Submit to law enforcement officers!
- Obey when they give you lawful orders!
- Be a cooperative and law-abiding citizen!

And the command as applied to government officials is likewise clear:

- Submit to lawful orders issued by your superiors!
- Obey and follow the law!
- Uphold and defend the constitution!

By God's command, *every person* is to be in submission. *No one is above the law.*

After giving this vital and comprehensive command, verse 1 goes on to explain why obedience in this area of life is so important: "For there is no authority except from God, and those which exist are established by God." The text could not be more clear: We must submit to government because its authority is *ordained by God.* And since their authority was delegated to them by God, rebellion against its agents is rebellion against God. So despising and rebelling against governmental authority brings punishment—not just from men, but also from God.

> Therefore whoever resists authority has opposed the ordinance of God; and they who have opposed will receive condemnation upon themselves.
> (Romans 13:2)

> . . . the Lord knows how to rescue the godly from tempta-
> tion, and to keep the unrighteous under punishment for the
> day of judgment, and especially those who indulge the flesh
> in its corrupt desires and despise authority.
> (2 Peter 2:9–10)

These two texts, as well as several others in Scripture, are clear: Despising authority is a characteristic of unbelievers and brings the wrath of God, for He is the source of all legitimate authority. Therefore, despising authority is a sure way of setting a life on a course to both temporal and eternal disaster.

As a consequence, it is vital that you view government and governing authorities *as having authority delegated to them from God.* As believers, we must heed the command of Romans 13:1: "Every person is to be in subjection to the governing authorities."

How should we view government?
Principle #2
We should view it as having authority delegated from God
(Romans 13:1–2).

Next, consider carefully Romans 13:3, where we find the third way we should view government:

> For rulers are not a cause of fear for good behavior, but for
> evil. Do you want to have no fear of authority? Do what is
> good and you will have praise from the same;
> (Romans 13:3)

Believers are clearly and repeatedly commanded by God in Holy Scripture to submit to governing authority. Why? Why would God command His people to submit to human governments? He did so because the authority of government was ordained by God to *restrain evil and reward good.*

If we stopped reading after verse 1 and verse 2, we might be tempted to wrongly conclude that the Bible teaches robotlike submission to governmental authority in all situations without any exceptions. But verse 3 reminds us that when God delegates authority, that authority must be used for its *divinely intended purpose*, and He sets strict limits on the legitimate use of that authority.

After the fall of mankind into sin, human government was given authority by God for a very good, kind, loving, and simple purpose. That purpose is clearly articulated in Romans 13:3—*to restrain evil and to protect good*. It is, therefore, wrong for human governments to misuse and abuse their authority by turning the divine purpose on its head.

> Woe to those who call evil good, and good evil; Who substitute darkness for light and light for darkness; Who substitute bitter for sweet and sweet for bitter!
> (Isaiah 5:20)

Now, in light of human history and experience, some people are confused as to why Romans 13:3 says that "rulers are not a cause of fear for good behavior, but for evil." How could Paul say that? After all, the ruler at this time was none other than Nero. And he often did the opposite of what is said here! How can verse 3 say that "rulers are not a cause of fear for good behavior," when Nero often was a cause of fear for good behavior? After all, he would frequently reward evil and punish good—doing the exact opposite of what verse 3 says.

The answer is that verse 3 is not talking about how things *were*, but how they *should* be. It is speaking about the divinely ordained *purpose* of every government, not the *actions* of every government. It is speaking about the perfection of the divine intent, not the imperfection of the human fulfillment. In other words, verse 3 is not an affirmation of the Roman government's *decisions*, but rather a description of its divinely mandated *responsibilities*. It is saying what its agents are *supposed* to do with the authority they have been given. And sadly, government officials—like all of humanity—often rebel against God by doing the exact opposite of what He ordained for them to do. Instead of restraining evil and protecting good, they begin facilitating evil and persecuting good.

Evil officials will answer to God for their rebellion against divine authority and for their misuse of the authority which He delegated to them. And in situations where government officials are facilitating evil and persecuting good, Christians not only do not have an obligation to submit to them, but also actually have an obligation *not* to submit to them. When governments abuse their power and exceed the limits of the authority God has delegated to them, *they themselves* are rebelling against God, and Christians *cannot* join them or support them in that rebellion. Christians must obey the *higher* authority—God rather than man. So verse 3 introduces a key premise:

> *God's purpose for government means there are limits to its*
> *authority.*

Now, along with that *premise*, there is also a *principle* here. Even someone as evil as Nero was nevertheless used by God to restrain evil. As crazy and wicked as Nero was, God was still using the Roman government to restrain evil. History shows that even in the worst and most corrupt administrations of the Roman empire, the government still punished thieves, murderers, and rapists. While those who governed were guilty of the evil of tyranny, they were nevertheless simultaneously being used by God to restrain the even greater evils of anarchy.

And so, as verses 3–4 teach, those who did acts of evil should indeed fear, for God was using the Roman government to bring vengeance down on the heads of such criminals. And the general principle stated here was true, even in Nero's Rome: Do good, and you don't need to live in fear of the authorities. Commit crimes, and you *should* fear, for, as verse 4 states, God hasn't placed a sword in their hand "for nothing."

Peter, in his discussion of government, makes an important distinction between *persecution* and *prosecution*:

> Keep your behavior excellent among the Gentiles, so that in
> the thing in which they slander you as evildoers, they may
> because of your good deeds, as they observe them, glorify
> God in the day of visitation. Submit yourselves for the Lord's
> sake to every human institution, whether to a king as the

one in authority, or to governors as sent by him for the punishment of evildoers and the praise of those who do right. For such is the will of God that by doing right you may silence the ignorance of foolish men. Act as free men, and do not use your freedom as a covering for evil, but use it as bondslaves of God. Honor all people, love the brotherhood, fear God, honor the king. Servants, be submissive to your masters with all respect, not only to those who are good and gentle, but also to those who are unreasonable. For this finds favor, if for the sake of conscience toward God a person bears up under sorrows when suffering unjustly. For what credit is there if, when you sin and are harshly treated, you endure it with patience? But if when you do what is right and suffer for it you patiently endure it, this finds favor with God. (1 Peter 2:12–20)

Peter is telling us that if we obey God rather than men, and are *persecuted* for it, this "finds favor with God." But if we commit crimes and are *prosecuted* as a result, we are being justly punished for disobeying the delegated authority God has given to governments.

So make sure you view government *as having a responsibility to restrain evil and protect good*. Then apply that view of government by obeying the command of Romans 13:3—"Do what is good."

How should we view government?
Principle #3
We should view it as having a responsibility to restrain evil and protect good (Romans 13:3).

The fourth way we should view government is found in verse 4:

. . . for it is a minister of God to you for good. But if you do what is evil, be afraid; for it does not bear the sword for nothing; for it is a minister of God, an avenger who brings wrath on the one who practices evil. (Romans 13:4)

This verse begins with an assertion that God ordained governmental authority for our good. Government "is a minister of God to you *for good.*" This is a vital point, and should always be kept in mind by the believer. The Lord's intent in ordaining and establishing government was good, kind, compassionate, and loving. Because of the total depravity of man, human suffering in this fallen world would be indescribably worse if God had not ordained government as a way of restraining evil.

Notice that twice in this verse, the phrase "minister of God" appears, using the Greek term *diakonos,* from which we also get our term "deacon." Just as a church deacon holds a specific office in the authority structure God ordained for the church, law enforcement holds a specific office in the authority structure God has ordained for society. Those who serve in this role are not just officers of the state; they are "ministers" of God.

Now, when most people think of a "minister of God," they think of someone like their pastor—somebody wearing a *tie* and carrying a *Bible.* But twice in this passage, God says He also has another type of minister—one who wears a *badge* and carries a *gun.* Both only have authority because it has been delegated to them by God. Both have limits to their authority imposed on them by God. But both are *ministers* of God. One is commissioned to *plead* with evildoers; the other is commissioned to *punish* evildoers. One *restores* sinners; the other *restrains* them. One *persuades* sinners not to sin; the other *punishes* them if they do. In other words, God gave one type of minister to society in order to *prevent* evil, and He gave the other to *punish* evil. One has a primarily *preventative* function, whereas the other has a primarily *punitive* function.

Therefore, lawbreakers and evildoers *should* be afraid, because the government doesn't bear the sword "for nothing." It bears the sword to *wield* it against evil. Governments—even pagan governments—are an instrument which God uses as "an avenger" who brings down God's wrath on those who practice evil.

> Woe to Assyria, the rod of My anger and the staff in whose hands is My indignation, I send it against a godless nation

and commission it against the people of My fury to capture booty and to seize plunder, and to trample them down like mud in the streets. Yet it does not so intend, nor does it plan so in its heart, but rather it is its purpose to destroy and to cut off many nations.
(Isaiah 10:5-7)

Just as God used Assyria as His "rod of anger" to punish godless Israel, He uses even evil governments as instruments of His wrath. So even an evil government can fulfill a good purpose—to restrain and punish evil.

So make sure you're viewing government *as a minister of God's wrath* toward evil. As a believer, you must heed the warning of Romans 13:4: "If you do what is evil, be afraid."

How should we view government?
Principle #4
We should view it as a minister of God's wrath (Romans 13:4).

Verse 5 directs us in the fifth way we should view government:

Therefore it is necessary to be in subjection, not only because of wrath, but also for conscience' sake.
(Romans 13:5)

When verse 5 says we should submit "for the sake of conscience," it is telling us that there is an important connection between the role of government and the role of the human conscience.

As John MacArthur has often pointed out, God has graciously provided four restraints on evil in this fallen world: the family, the conscience, the government, and the church. Three of those restraints are external, and one—the conscience—is internal. Later on, we will consider the three external restraints in greater detail. But for now, building on Dr. MacArthur's teaching on this topic, I want to make a few brief comments about each of those four restraints:

THE FAMILY: The "first commandment with a promise" is for children to obey their parents. We are born with a sin nature, and the first restraint on human depravity which a child encounters is a parent saying, "No, no," when he throws a fit or takes a toy from another child. God's design is for children to receive their first lesson about the consequences of sin via the loving discipline of their mom and dad. God has ordained parents to be the first line of defense against human evil.

THE CONSCIENCE: Romans 2:15 says that the law of God has been written on the heart of every person, and that the conscience either accuses or defends a person based upon whether or not he or she keeps God's law. As children grow up and become more and more independent from their parents, the role of the conscience becomes more and more important. Since it is the only *internal* restraint on evil for unregenerate people, a strong and well-informed conscience is absolutely vital to every person, and to all of society. The conscience is a key restraining influence on human evil, but it is not infallible, and it can be seared, misinformed, or suppressed.

THE GOVERNMENT: God has provided armed reinforcements for the conscience by giving the sword to government. So, as verse 5 says, we should submit to government "for conscience' sake." When we submit to government, we obey God's law, and our conscience affirms that righteous choice. When we rebel against divinely ordained authority, we violate and suppress the conscience. And when people have suppressed the *internal* restraint of their conscience, they need an *external* restraint. Government is designed by God to bring physical power and external authority to bear when evil has not been restrained by an individual's conscience.

THE CHURCH: The church is the body of Christ and "the pillar and support of the truth" (1 Timothy 3:15). We are "salt and light" (Matthew 5:13–16). Salt was a preservative that kept things from rotting, and light shows people the right path. So the church has an *essential* role in society, and that role is still as vital to modern society as salt and light were to ancient societies.

These four restraints on evil—the family, the conscience, the government, and the church—are elements of God's common grace to a fallen world. So unsurprisingly, those four restraints are *hated* by Satan, for they stand between him and the fulfillment of his evil schemes. And so he relentlessly *attacks* them:

- The sexual revolution and the feminist and LGBTQ movements are an attack on God's design for the *family*.
- The filth being cranked out by the entertainment industry along with the immoral lifestyles of so many political, educational, and religious leaders is searing the *conscience* of our nation.
- Both the abuse of authority as well as the disdain for authority which we are seeing almost daily on the news are satanic attacks on the restraining bulwark of *government*.
- And of course, Satan continually wars against the *church*, both by sending infiltrators to discredit it from inside, and persecutors to destroy it from outside.

Satan's ultimate goal is the complete domination of evil in this world which accompanies the rise of the Antichrist. And for that to happen, one by one those four restraints need to crumble. But Satan has a problem: he cannot prevail against the church, for Jesus said, "I will build My church, and the gates of hell will not prevail against it" (Matthew 16:18).

And so, as long as the church is in the way, there will be at least some restraint on evil in this world. The Holy Spirit is mentioned in 2 Thessalonians 2:6 as the One who "restrains" the "man of lawlessness." The reason the church exercises such a powerful restraint on evil is not because it has political power or social influence, but because its people are indwelled by the Holy Spirit. Christians restrain evil because they are indwelled by *The Restrainer*.

But there is coming a day when the Lord will determine that enough is enough, and He will rapture the church. When that happens, *The Restrainer*—the indwelling Holy Spirit—"will be taken out of the way." 2 Thessalonians 2 makes it clear what will happen once that final restraint is removed: apostasy and the rise of the Antichrist.

Therefore, when we see that all four restraints on evil are under attack, we should *get extremely serious* about the Great Commission, for, as Jesus said, "We must work the works of Him who sent Me as long as it is day; night is coming when no one can work" (John 9:4). We need to be busily working in God's harvest fields while we still can, for "now is the day of salvation" (2 Corinthians 6:2).

There is coming a day when the church age will end, and the restraining influence of the body of Christ will be gone. But until then, the four restraints God has ordained are operating, and they are a manifestation of His kindness, love, and grace to a fallen world. Therefore, believers should strongly defend the right of parents to discipline their children, for that is the vital first line of defense against evil. Christians should do everything possible to inform and strengthen the conscience of the nation, serving in and through their local church. Believers serving in government should be exemplary in both character and job performance. And every believer should be grateful for the restraining influence of government, submitting to the authorities "for the sake of conscience." For when someone ignores the *internal* pangs of conscience, the *external* pains of the government's sword provide a safeguard against unrestrained evil.

So make sure you're viewing government *as a safeguard for when the human conscience fails.* Believers must heed the teaching of Romans 13:5: "It is necessary to be in subjection . . . for conscience' sake."

How should we view government?
Principle #5
We should view it as a safeguard for when the human conscience
fails (Romans 13:5).

The sixth way we should view government is found in Romans 13:6:

For because of this you also pay taxes, for rulers are servants of God, devoting themselves to this very thing.
(Romans 13:6)

At the end of verse 6, Paul calls the rulers "servants of God" (*leitourgoi Theou*). I don't think most modern readers realize how radical the phrase *servants of God* was in the context of first-century Rome. Keep in mind that Nero thought he *was* God, and everyone else were *his* servants. To that idolatrous notion, Paul says an emphatic *no* in verse 6. Even the emperor himself is just a *servant*. He, too, is under a higher authority, for he, like all rulers, is merely a *servant* of God!

Human rulers often think they are *masters of men*, but really they are just *servants of God*. And a servant must obey the will and the laws of his master. Even the mightiest human ruler is just a servant of Almighty God!

In other words, human rulers *do* have authority delegated to them by God, but they do *not* have absolute authority. They have *delegated* authority, not *inherent* authority. They are accountable to the higher law and higher authority of God, for they are servants of God, not masters of men.

So make sure that you are viewing government officials *as servants of God,* not *masters of men.* As a believer, you must remember that government is not your highest authority, for as Romans 13:6 says, "Rulers are servants of God."

How should we view government?
Principle #6
We should view it as made up of servants of God, not as masters
of men (Romans 13:6).

The seventh way this passage directs us to view government is found in verse 7:

> Render to all what is due them: tax to whom tax is due; custom to whom custom; fear to whom fear; honor to whom honor.
> (Romans 13:7)

By using the word "render," Paul makes a very clear allusion to the words of Jesus in Mark 12:17:

And Jesus said to them, "Render to Caesar the things that are Caesar's, and to God the things that are God's." And they were amazed at Him.
(Mark 12:17)

In both Mark 12 and Romans 13, we are told that we have a responsibility to *render* to Caesar that which is Caesar's. Both passages specifically state that *taxes* are Caesar's, and Romans 13 adds that *custom, fear,* and *honor* also belong to Caesar.

So, let me ask you this question: Are you rendering to Caesar that which is Caesar's? There are several points of application that may be involved in this.

- Are you filing your tax return with complete honesty?
- Do you speak and act with respect toward governing authorities—whether the law enforcement officer who pulls you over, the city zoning office, judges, your state and federal representatives, your governor, or your president?
- Do you honor them because of the office they hold, even if you dislike them as a person or disagree with their policies?

If this is something you are not doing, then you need to *render* to Caesar that which *God* says is due to Caesar—taxes, honor, and respect—and you need to *render* to God that which is *God's*.

In the next section, we'll be discussing how to distinguish between what comes under the jurisdiction of *Caesar* and that which is more specifically *God's*. But the point I want to drive home right now is that Scripture calls us to be not just *good* citizens, but *model* citizens who exemplify honor, respect, and submission to the authorities God has sovereignly placed over us.

It is vitally important for you to make sure you're viewing government authorities *with appropriate respect* and that you are giving them *appropriate honor*. As a believer, you must heed the command of Romans 13:7: "Render to all what is due them."

How should we view government?
Principle #7

We should view it with appropriate respect and give its members appropriate honor (Romans 13:7).

Before we transition, let's summarize what we've learned in this first section. We've been studying Romans 12:14–13:7 to find answers to the question "What should a believer's attitude and perspective be toward human government?" From this passage, we've established seven ways in which we should view the governing authorities over us.

- They are individuals with eternal souls;
- They have authority delegated from God;
- They have a responsibility to restrain evil and to protect good;
- They serve as a minister of God's wrath;
- They are a safeguard for when human conscience fails;
- They are servants of God, not masters of men;
- They deserve appropriate respect and honor.

May the Lord help you to view government the way our good God tells us to—not the way political pundits tell us to. That isn't easy, but if the Christians living in Rome under the rule of Nero could do it, then so can you—no matter what may be coming.

Here's the key takeaway from the first section of this study:

Scripture calls us to be good citizens who honor, respect, and submit to the authorities God has sovereignly placed over us.

In Jeremiah 29:7, the Israelites were instructed to "seek the welfare of the city where I have sent you into exile, and pray to the LORD on its behalf; for in its welfare you will have welfare." Likewise, all Christians should seek the welfare of the country where God has sovereignly placed them, and pray to the Lord on its behalf. Christians should *love* their country, and they should be *model citizens* in all respects—including in the way they honor, respect, and submit to their governing authorities.

2

When to Submit and When to Obey

How can we know when we are supposed to submit to government (Romans 13:1), and when we must "obey God rather than men" (Acts 5:29)?

We concluded the first section with Romans 13:7, which instructs us to "[r]ender to all what is due them: tax to whom tax is due; custom to whom custom; fear to whom fear; honor to whom honor." As I already mentioned, Paul's use of the word *render* in Romans 13:7 is a clear allusion to the words of Jesus in Mark 12:17, so we will now consider that key verse again:

> And Jesus said to them, "Render to Caesar the things that are Caesar's, and to God the things that are God's." And they were amazed at Him.
> (Mark 12:17)

In this section, we will consider an important and extremely practical question: *How can we distinguish between that which is Caesar's and that which is God's?*

In other words, how can we distinguish between situations when God wants us to submit to government, and when He wants us to follow the example of the apostles in obeying God rather than men? What are the limits God has placed on human authority? And how can we know when those lines have been crossed and we must therefore obey God rather than men?

How we answer those questions will depend on our theological beliefs, so it is important we get our theology—our understanding of what the Bible teaches about God—right. And to get our theology right, we need to build it on the foundation of Scripture, not our personal, political, or cultural biases. There are seven core convictions about the Bible, the Word of God, which must guide the formation of our theology:

1. Inspiration: God said it.
2. Inerrancy: What God said is true.
3. Preservation: What God said hasn't been lost.
4. Perspicuity: What God said is clear.
5. Authority: What God said is binding.
6. Sufficiency: What God said is all we need.
7. Historical-Grammatical Hermeneutics: We must honor God's authorial intent.

Those seven convictions aren't just academic or theoretical; rather, they are eminently practical. Our convictions regarding the Bible shape the process by which we form our theology, and our theology shapes our lives.

Any building necessarily has to have a foundation if the structure is to be robust and to remain intact. I sometimes use the analogy of the building of a pyramid—in this instance, a "theological pyramid." As believers following the Word of God faithfully, the "theological pyramid" is a way of illustrating how our theological beliefs are firmly founded on the Holy Word of God. In outline, it involves four steps.

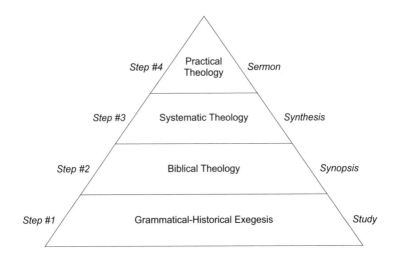

The Process of Grammatical-Historical Exegesis

• •

STEP 1: Proper Hermeneutics and Exegesis
- Lexical Analysis (What is the precise meaning of the words themselves?)
- Syntactical Analysis (What is the precise significance of the grammar?)
- Near Context (How is this text connected to and explained by what immediately precedes and follows it?)
- Far Context (How is this passage connected to the message of the chapter, the book, and the whole Bible?)
- Historical Context (Whom was this written by, whom was it first written for, when was it written, and why?)

STEP 2: Proper Biblical Theology
- Author's Theological Intent (What was the author's intended theological point?)
- Author's Practical Intent (What was the author's intended practical application?)
- Synopsis of Authorial Intent (How did the author intend this text to affect our desires, thoughts, words, and actions?)

STEP 3: Proper Systematic Theology
- Consistency of Interpretation (Is your view consistent with the rest of Scripture? Have you considered the whole counsel of God?)
- Boundaries of Interpretation: (Are you stopping short or going beyond what is written? Have you slipped into either legalism or antinomianism? Have you drifted from historic Christian orthodoxy or orthopraxy?)

STEP 4: Proper Application
- Personal Obedience (Loving the Lord by "keeping His commandments" and giving Him "first place in everything.")
- Public Witness (Loving the lost by "speaking the truth in love" and keeping the gospel "of first importance.")

As may be seen in the diagram, each of these steps is logical and sequential, moving through the fourfold process of study, synopsis, synthesis, and service to Christ.

With this set of principles in place, let us now apply this process (albeit in a much abbreviated and simplified form) to the questions we're asking about governmental authority. We will briefly exegete five key texts (step #1), glean five principles from them (step #2), put those five principles together into a systematic view of the key areas of authority God has established (step #3), and then suggest some practical applications (step #4).

Key Verse 1: Matthew 28:18

The first key verse we'll study is Matthew 28:18, which is the opening verse of the Great Commission which the Lord gave to the church just before His ascension.

> And Jesus came up and spoke to them, saying, "All authority has been given to Me in heaven and on earth.
> (Matthew 28:18)

We must consider a key word which has *huge* significance for our topic: Notice the word "all" in verse 18: "*All* authority. . . ."

Jesus begins His Great Commission to the church by asserting that He has *unlimited* and *ultimate* authority—both in heaven and on earth. He is the KING of all kings and the LORD of all lords (Revelation 19:16). He has "*all* authority in heaven and on earth," for He is *one* with the Father (John 10:30).

Our Triune God—Father, Son, and Holy Spirit—is *all-powerful* and absolutely *sovereign.* Psalm 115:3 states that "Our God is in heaven. He does whatever He pleases." And Psalm 135:6 records, "Whatever the LORD pleases, He does, in heaven and in earth, in the seas and in all deeps."

God is *sovereign* over *all*—including governments. Proverbs 21:1 states that "The king's heart is like channels of water in the hand of the LORD; He turns it wherever He wishes." Daniel 2:20–21a says, "Let the name of God be blessed forever and ever, For wisdom and power belong to Him. It is He who changes the times

and the epochs; He removes kings and establishes kings. . . ."
Moreover, in John 19:10–11 it is written:

> So Pilate said to Him, "You do not speak to me? Do You not know that I have authority to release You, and I have authority to crucify You?" Jesus answered, "You would have no authority over Me, unless it had been given you from above; for this reason he who delivered Me to you has the greater sin."
> (John 19:10–11)

Jesus tells Pilate the same thing that is recorded in Romans 13:1–2, namely that the authority which government wields has been *delegated* by God. Since that authority is *delegated* authority (not *inherent* authority), it is *limited* authority and not *absolute* authority. And the officers who exercise that authority are accountable to God to fulfill the purpose for which He gave them authority—namely, *to restrain evil* and *to reward good*.

So as we think through issues of authority, we need to always remember that *all* authority, in heaven and on earth, *belongs* to Jesus Christ. Therefore, all other authorities are *subordinate* to Him, and their authority is *limited* by Him.

Key Principle Derived from Matthew 28:18
(1)
Since only God has unlimited authority, all delegated authority is limited authority.

We see biblical examples of this principle when the Lord judges Nebuchadnezzar, Belshazzar, and other kings and kingdoms for exalting themselves, exceeding the divine limits on their glory and authority, and refusing to honor and obey God.

Key Verse 2: Matthew 28:19

> And Jesus came up and spoke to them, saying, "All authority has been given to Me in heaven and on earth. Go therefore and make disciples of all the nations, baptizing them in the

name of the Father and the Son and the Holy Spirit, teaching them to observe all that I commanded you; and lo, I am with you always, even to the end of the age."
(Matthew 28:18-20)

Earlier, I pointed out the importance of the word *all* in verse 18: "*All* authority...has been given to Me." Now I want to draw your attention to the second time the word *all* appears in the Great Commission: ". . .teaching them to observe *all* that I've commanded you" (v. 20a).

These two uses of the word *all* in the Great Commission are connected by the word *therefore* in verse 19. Why are we to obey *all* that Christ commands? Because *all* authority belongs to Him. "*All* authority has been given to Me. . .therefore, go and make disciples, baptizing them, and teaching them to obey *all* I've commanded. . . ." *Jesus*, the highest authority, has commanded us to obey *all* He has commanded, and has instructed us to teach others to do the same.

The Lord expects full obedience from His people. And full obedience has two components: We must do everything that He commands, and we must not do anything which He forbids. If we do something which God forbids, we sin by *commission* (what we do). If we do not do something He has commanded us to do, we sin by *omission* (what we fail to do). Both sins of *commission* and *omission* are evil.

Therefore, if a government by law or edict tries to force believers to do something which God clearly forbids—a sin of commission—the believer must obey God rather than men. Likewise, if a government by law or edict tries to prohibit believers from obeying a clear command of God—a sin of omission—the believer must obey God rather than men. "Teach them," Jesus said, "to obey *all* that I have commanded you."

Key Principle Derived from Matthew 28:19
(2)
Governments exceed their delegated authority when they either require disobedience against God, or when they restrict obedience to God.

Examples of this principle are found throughout the Bible. In the Old Testament, the Hebrew midwives refused to submit to Pharaoh's order to kill newborn male children, for this would have violated the sixth commandment and thus been a *sin of commission*. In the New Testament, the apostles in Acts 4–5 refused to submit to governmental orders to stop preaching the gospel, for to do so would have been a *sin of omission*.

But perhaps the clearest example of this principle is that seen in the life of Daniel. When wicked officials convinced the king to make a law that no one could pray to anyone except the king, Daniel continued his practice of praying to God and God alone three times a day...and faced the lions' den as a result. He refused to commit a *sin of omission* by ceasing to pray, and he refused to commit a *sin of commission* by praying to the king instead of God.

Key Verse 3: Mark 12:17

> And Jesus said to them, "Render to Caesar the things that are Caesar's, and to God the things that are God's." And they were amazed at Him.
> (Mark 12:17)

In the analogy of our theological pyramid, we mentioned how important *context* is to proper exegesis, and this verse is no exception. Consider the preceding context:

> Then they sent some of the Pharisees and Herodians to Him in order to trap Him in a statement. They came and said to Him, "Teacher, we know that You are truthful and defer to no one; for You are not partial to any, but teach the way of God in truth. Is it lawful to pay a poll-tax to Caesar, or not? Shall we pay or shall we not pay?" But He, knowing their hypocrisy, said to them, "Why are you testing Me? Bring Me a denarius to look at."
> (Mark 12:13–15)

In verse 15, it states that Jesus knew their *hypocrisy*. As verse 13 already stated, it wasn't even an honest question—it was a *trap*.

But there is another sense in which the Pharisees and Herodians were being hypocritical. Elsewhere, Jesus had confronted them for giving God their money but withholding their *hearts*:

> "But woe to you Pharisees! For you pay tithe of mint and rue and every kind of garden herb, and yet disregard justice and the love of God; but these are the things you should have done without neglecting the others."
> (Luke 11:42)

Again and again, Jesus had rebuked the Pharisees for their hollow, superficial, hypocritical religiosity. And here they were again (see Mark 12:14), asking whether or not they owed Caesar their money, when the real issue was that they owed God their hearts.

Their whole way of thinking about these issues was driven by their spiritual hypocrisy. They were so focused on debating *material things* that they were ignoring *spiritual things*. They were debating what they should give to Caesar while completely ignoring what they should give to God.

So Jesus confronted their hypocrisy in a *powerful* way:

> They brought [a denarius]. And He said to them, "Whose likeness and inscription is this?" And they said to Him, "Caesar's." And Jesus said to them, "Render to Caesar the things that are Caesar's, and to God the things that are God's." And they were amazed at Him.
> (Mark 12:16–17)

When Jesus asked, "Whose *likeness* is this?" He was using the same terminology used to describe the creation of man in the image and likeness of God as recorded in Genesis 1. It is as if He was saying, "This piece of metal bears Caesar's likeness, so give it to him. But *you* bear *God's likeness*, so give *yourself* to Him." That which bears Caesar's image and likeness belongs to Caesar; but that which bears God's image and likeness belongs to God.

Jesus tells the hypocritical Pharisees, "Taxes belong to Caesar so give them to him. But *you* belong to God, so give yourselves to

Him." In other words, just as Caesar has the right to receive *taxes*, God has the right to receive *worship*.

This has *huge* implications for a proper theological understanding of government: It means that Caesar can indeed legitimately lay a claim to people's money, but only God can lay claim to the people themselves. In other words, Caesar can demand our *wealth*, but he cannot demand our *worship*.

Yes, government has *taxation* authority, but, no, government does not have *total* authority. As we considered in Principle 1, governments have *delegated* authority, and delegated authority is always *limited* in its rights and powers. What is God's belongs to God, and a lower authority has no right to steal worship from God or to hinder God from receiving the worship due His glorious majesty. Government has no right to stand between the worshipper and the One who alone is worthy of worship. Worship is not just a "right" guaranteed to American citizens by the United States constitution; it is a spiritual *obligation* commanded by the Most High. Worship is not optional. As Psalm 29:2 says, "Ascribe to the LORD the glory due to His name; Worship the LORD in holy array."

Key Principle Derived from Mark 12:17
(3)
Governments exceed their authority when they either demand worship, or prevent worship.

The most poignant biblical example of authorities *demanding* worship was when Shadrach, Meshach, and Abednego faced the fiery furnace rather than obey the king's command to bow down and worship an idol. See Daniel 3:8–25.

The most poignant example of authorities trying to *prevent* worship is found in Luke 19:37–40. When the Pharisees tell Jesus to make the people stop praising Him, Jesus replied, "I tell you, if these become silent, the stones will cry out!"

Key Verse 4: Ephesians 5:23

For the husband is the head of the wife, as Christ also is the head of the church, He Himself being the Savior of the body. (Ephesians 5:23)

This verse succinctly states what is taught in dozens of other passages: Christ is the *Head* of the church, and the husband is the *head* of the home. God is a God of order, and He has established clear authority structures in the church and in the family:

- In the *family*, children are to obey their parents, and the wife is to submit to her husband, because he is the head of the home.
- In the *church*, members are to submit to the elders, and elders are to submit to the Word of God, for Christ is the Head of the church.

Throughout the New Testament, and particularly in the letter to the Ephesians, the exclusive headship of Christ over the church is repeatedly emphasized:

And He put all things in subjection under His feet, and gave Him as head over all things to the church, which is His body, the fullness of Him who fills all in all. (Ephesians 1:22–23)

[B]ut speaking the truth in love, we are to grow up in all aspects into Him who is the head, even Christ, from whom the whole body, being fitted and held together by what every joint supplies, according to the proper working of each individual part, causes the growth of the body for the building up of itself in love. (Ephesians 4:15–16)

Wives, be subject to your own husbands, as to the Lord. For the husband is the head of the wife, as Christ also is the head of the church, He Himself being the Savior of the body. But as the church is subject to Christ, so also the wives ought to be to their husbands in everything. (Ephesians 5:22–24)

So it is vital to remember that Christ, not Caesar, is the Head of the church. The state does *not* have the right to rule over the church or regulate its worship, for headship over the church has *not* been given to government. It is biblically qualified elders—not government officials—who have been ordained by Christ, the Head of the church, to be His under-shepherds and overseers. *Likewise, it is the husband, not the state, who is the head of the family.* The state does *not* have the right to redefine marriage, nor does it have the right to intrude on parental authority in the home. It is *parents*, not government agencies, who have been given the authority and the responsibility to raise children in the fear and admonition of the Lord. The village doesn't raise children; parents do!

Key Principle Derived from Ephesians 5:23
(4)
Governments exceed their delegated authority when they intrude on authority God has delegated exclusively to the church or to the family.

Stated differently, government is not the head of the church, and government is not the head of the family.

A poignant example of God rebuking a civil authority for intruding on the exclusive domain of a spiritual authority is found in 1 Samuel 13, where King Saul is punished by God for offering sacrifices himself instead of waiting for the prophet Samuel.

And a poignant example of God rebuking a civil authority for intruding on the exclusive domain of a husband is found in the tragic example of David using his governmental authority to get rid of Uriah, in order to take Bathsheba for himself (see 2 Samuel 11:14–25).

Key Verse: Acts 5:29

But Peter and the apostles answered, "We must obey God rather than men."
(Acts 5:29)

For fuller context, consider the words of chapter 4 in review:

> And when they had summoned them, they commanded them not to speak or teach at all in the name of Jesus. But Peter and John answered and said to them, "Whether it is right in the sight of God to give heed to you rather than to God, you be the judge; for we cannot stop speaking about what we have seen and heard."
> (Acts 4:18–20)

> But someone came and reported to them, "The men whom you put in prison are standing in the temple and teaching the people!" Then the captain went along with the officers and proceeded to bring them back without violence (for they were afraid of the people, that they might be stoned). When they had brought them, they stood them before the Council. The high priest questioned them, saying, "We gave you strict orders not to continue teaching in this name, and yet, you have filled Jerusalem with your teaching and intend to bring this man's blood upon us." But Peter and the apostles answered, "We must obey God rather than men."
> (Acts 5:25–29)

These crucial passages bring us full circle: We started our study of these five key texts by noting that the Great Commission says that *all* authority in heaven and on earth belongs to Jesus Christ. And we also noted that the Great Commission commands the church to teach people to obey *all* that Jesus has commanded.

Therefore, when governments do things such as (a) require disobedience against God, or restrict obedience to God. . . (b) when they demand worship or prevent worship. . . (c) when they intrude on the exclusive authority of the church or the family. . . then we must, as the apostles said, "obey God rather than men."

Key Principle Derived from Acts 5:29
(5)
When governments exceed their delegated authority, believers have both the right and the duty to obey God rather than men.

We see examples of this principle throughout Scripture. Consider the examples below:

- When Pharaoh commanded the Hebrew midwives to kill every male child, they rightly refused. (See Exodus 1:15–21.)
- Rahab rightly refused the demand of her governing authorities that she turn in the Israelite spies. (See Joshua 2:1–6.)
- Elijah exercised his spiritual authority in opposition to the civil authority of wicked king Ahab and his even more wicked queen, Jezebel. (See 1 Kings 18:16–24.)
- Shadrach, Meschach, Abednego, Daniel, the apostles, and many others faced situations where they could not submit to government without disobeying God. (See Daniel 3:16–28.)
- Paul was beaten, imprisoned, put on trial, and eventually executed because of his resolve to obey God rather than men. (See 2 Timothy 4:7–8.)

So there are numerous biblical examples of believers "obeying God rather than men." And those examples can be grouped into three broad categories. Christians must obey God rather than men:

1. When governments require disobedience against God, or restrict obedience to God;
2. When governments demand worship or prevent worship;
3. When governments intrude on the authority God has given exclusively to the church or to the family.

Reviewing the Thinking Process

As we endeavor to navigate the complex issues of authority and responsibility, here is a review and synopsis of the ground we have covered.

STUDY

So far, following step #1 in our "theological pyramid," we've studied five key verses: Matthew 28:18, Matthew 28:19, Mark 12:17, Ephesians 5:23, and Acts 5:29.

SYNOPSIS

Then, following step #2, we've derived a synopsis of biblical teaching consisting of Five Key Principles of a Biblical Theology of Government:

- Since *only* God has unlimited authority, all *delegated* authority is *limited* authority.
- Governments exceed their delegated authority when they either *require* disobedience against God, or when they *restrict* obedience to God.
- Governments exceed their authority when they either *demand* worship, or *prevent* worship.
- Governments exceed their delegated authority when they *intrude* on authority God has delegated exclusively to the *church* or the *family*.
- When governments exceed their delegated authority, believers have both the *right* and the *duty* to obey God rather than men.

SYNTHESIS

In the next part of this book, we will proceed to step #3 of our theological pyramid, and formulate a systematic synthesis derived from what we've learned. We will then be in a position to consider how to know when the government has exceeded the limits of its divinely ordained authority and intruded on the jurisdiction which God has given exclusively to the church or to the family.

3

Identifying Government Overreach and Intrusion

How can we know when the government has exceeded the limits of its divinely ordained authority and intruded on authority which God has given exclusively to the church or to the family?

The Bible is clear in its teaching that God is a God of *order*. In His love, in His kindness, and in His wisdom, He has established three primary jurisdictions of external authority in order to restrain evil, to reward good, and to facilitate the expansion of the gospel throughout the world. These three jurisdictions are:

1. The Family;
2. The Government;
3. The Church.

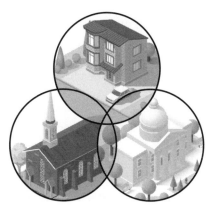

Earlier, we introduced three *external* spheres of authority, and one *internal* safeguard (the conscience), which God has graciously ordained to restrain evil in this fallen world. We will now take a closer look at why each one of the three overlapping areas of external authority is so important in God's design, and why each one is such a blessing to mankind.

1) *The Family*

I've listed the family first, because it was the first to be established by God as recorded in Genesis 2:24. In fact, it is the only one of the three that existed in the garden of Eden before the fall of man into sin. And of course, if there were no sin, there would be no need for God to place a sword—the symbol and instrument of power—in the hand of government. There would also be no need for the church, for there would be no need for ambassadors if people didn't need to be reconciled to God. So it is rightly said that the family is the first and foundational building block of society.

God ordained the family to be the primary provider of love, shelter, nurture, and care in society. And He also ordained the family to be the first line of defense in the battle to restrain human evil. God graciously gave parents the *rod* before He ever gave government the *sword*.

If you are a parent, it is not loving or merciful to deprive your children of discipline by withholding the *rod*, because that means the first real instrument of discipline they will otherwise encounter is the government's *sword*. When parents withhold the *rod*, they put their children on a collision course with the *sword*. A child whose sin nature isn't restrained by his *parents* will have to have his sin nature restrained by the *police*. Getting a few swats to the bottom can save a child from a lifetime of misery—or even from death.

> He who withholds his rod hates his son,
> But he who loves him disciplines him diligently.
> (Proverbs 13:24)

> Discipline your son while there is hope,
> And do not desire his death.
> (Proverbs 19:18)

> Foolishness is bound up in the heart of a child;
> The rod of discipline will remove it far from him.
> (Proverbs 22:15)

Do not hold back discipline from the child,
Although you strike him with the rod, he will not die.
You shall strike him with the rod
And rescue his soul from Sheol.

(Proverbs 23:13–14)

Our godless society increasingly looks at parental discipline as a curse rather than as a blessing—as something bad rather something good. But God's Word is clear that parental discipline is both *necessary* and *good*, because the most dangerous threat to a child is his own sin. It is *sin* which destroys. It is *sin* which robs a child of the abundant life God desires for him. And it is *sin* which produces death and judgment. Therefore, loving, controlled, and appropriate parental discipline is a gift of love which parents are *commanded* by God to give to their children. And as Scripture says, those who withhold it *hate* their children (see Proverbs 13:24), for they do nothing to restrain the evil which kills, steals, and destroys.

As a parent, you should not let your kids blow through the restraint of parental authority without consequences. If *you* won't restrain the encroachment of evil with a few swats to the bottom, *either* someone else will restrain it or your child will face the natural and inevitable consequences of sin. And *both* of those are much, much worse than a spanking administered properly and in love by a godly parent.

Key Summary Point:
Family is the first area of authority ordained by God to restrain evil, but it is not the only area of authority.

2) The Government

As I have already mentioned, in Eden, before the fall, there was no sin and therefore no need to restrain it. But after the fall, humanity was plunged into a never-ending cycle of unrestrained violence and evil. So, as recorded in Genesis 9, God established government and placed a sword in its hand with these words: "Whoever sheds man's blood, by man his blood shall be shed, for in the image of God He made man" (Genesis 9:6). As Romans

13:1–2 says, government is *established* by God, and as Romans 13:3–4 says, God gave government a *sword* to restrain evil and to bring vengeance on evildoers. So government was established by God after the fall of man into sin, in order to restrain evil and protect the innocent.

By the way, this is why *anarchy* is so *anachronistic*. Anarchists naïvely think that if we could just get rid of all human authority, we would all be living in a utopia of love and freedom. They seem to believe that the only thing standing in between us and a return to the garden of Eden is the abolition of governing authority. If man was perfect, sinless, and good, they might have a point—for there was indeed no need for a human government to bear the sword in Eden. But when mankind fell into sin, such a scenario was no longer possible.

> Then the LORD saw that the wickedness of man was great on the earth, and that every intent of the thoughts of his heart was only evil continually.
> (Genesis 6:5)

> . . .as it is written, "There is none righteous, not even one; there is none who understands, there is none who seeks for God; all have turned aside, together they have become useless; there is none who does good, there is not even one." "Their throat is an open grave, with their tongues they keep deceiving," "the poison of asps is under their lips"; "whose mouth is full of cursing and bitterness"; "their feet are swift to shed blood, destruction and misery are in their paths, and the path of peace they have not known." "There is no fear of God before their eyes."
> (Romans 3:10–18)

The teaching of Scripture is clear: Mankind is totally depraved. So it is silly, childish, and naïve to think that the removal of the restraining power of government will produce peace, love, and harmony. What anarchy actually produces is the chaos, senseless violence, and suffering depicted so well in William Golding's famous novel, *Lord of the Flies*.

But *anarchy* isn't just naïve and foolish; it is also the partner and best friend of *tyranny*.

When a society descends into anarchy, the chaos and lawlessness leads the population to desperation, and desperation leads the people to willingly accept tyranny in exchange for some semblance of order and safety—even if that "new order" is oppressive. And of course, it is the oppression and atrocities which always accompany tyranny which eventually make subsequent generations willing to support rebellions by anarchist radicals. A vicious cycle of anarchy, tyranny, anarchy, tyranny is the sad but predictable result.

Tyranny and anarchy are evil twins. While the clothing they wear may be very different, if you look more closely you'll see their similarities, for *anarchy* is really just *tyranny* on a smaller scale. Instead of one big tyrant ruling a nation, anarchy brings about thousands of little tyrants, each of whom rules a neighborhood or a street. In both situations, the population is ruled by dictators— whether one for a whole country, or one per city block.

So a Christian worldview opposes *both* tyranny and anarchy, and instead supports the biblical principle of *limited government*. As we have learned, if government's authority is a *delegated* authority, it cannot be an *absolute* authority. Delegated authority is, by definition, *limited authority*—and that is where we get the important principle of *limited government* from.

Key Summary Point:
Government is the second area of authority ordained by God to restrain evil and promote good.

3) The Church

If God gave parents the *rod,* and if He gave governments the *sword,* then what did He give to the church to fulfill *its* role in restraining evil? The answer is that He gave the *shepherd's staff.* Christ, the Head of the church, is the *Good Shepherd.* And He has given pastors and elders spiritual authority and ordained them to serve as His under-shepherds. In fact, the word *pastor* comes from the Greek *poimen,* which simply means *shepherd.*

As Christ's under-shepherds, pastors and elders are responsible to feed the flock, to care for it, and to lead it. And, as recorded in Matthew 18, Hebrews 12, and several other passages, Jesus specifically commanded that a core aspect of pastoral care for the flock is *church discipline*. When a sheep goes astray or creates a division in the flock, a pastor must use the hook on his staff to lovingly but firmly pull that sheep back into the safety and fellowship of the fold. He must do so gently, do so in love, and do so according to the written Word of Christ, the Great Shepherd. But he *must* do so. Christ commands and requires it.

Key Summary Point:
The Church is the third area of authority ordained by God. Christ is the head of the church.

In summary, in the big picture, God has ordained three areas or jurisdictions of authority: family authority, governmental authority, and spiritual authority. All three have been given a symbol and means of discipline:

- the *family* was given the *rod;*
- the *government* was given the *sword;*
- the *church* was given the *staff.*

All three are gracious gifts to humanity, for their purpose is to restrain evil and to promote good.

Satan well knows this. And so attacking these three jurisdictions of authority is a core part of his strategy. As a result, he is often successful in *corrupting* either the family, the church, or the government, bringing about abuse in one or more of these areas. However, it is in such situations that the wisdom of God's design becomes apparent. Because each area has been given authority by God, a system of checks and balances was created which makes it difficult for Satan to gain complete, unrestrained control of a society.

4

Checks and Balances

The Analogy of the Traffic Lights

Let's discuss how that system of checks and balances is designed to work, using the illustration of traffic lights.

THE RED-LIGHT PRINCIPLE

• • • • • • • • • • • • • • • • •

All of these three jurisdictions have areas of authority that are their *exclusive domain.*

How do we determine what belongs in each area's "exclusive domain"?

We study Scripture to see what God commands, instructs, authorizes, or requires of one area of authority, but does not command, instruct, authorize, or require of any other area of authority.

At an intersection, if a miscalibrated traffic light intrudes on the exclusive authority of another traffic light, a vehicle collision is certain to follow—with disastrous results.

Likewise, the concept of *exclusive domain* is important, because if one sphere of authority intrudes on the exclusive domain of another, disorder, suffering, and evil inevitably result.

Consider, for example, what happened when the church merged with the state or when the church dominated the state: the Holy Roman Empire wasn't very holy.

Or consider those horrible examples from recent years when churches discovered that predatory wolves had infiltrated the flock and sexually abused their little lambs—but they decided to "handle it internally" rather than report the crimes to the police. That is a very good example of the church *intruding* on the exclusive domain of the government, for it is the *government*—not the church—to whom God has given the sword to bring vengeance on evildoers and criminals. When a church fails to refer crimes to the proper authorities, it is sinning by exceeding its authority and intruding into the realm of the exclusive authority of the government.

Or, consider what happens when a church slips into *legalism*: The church inevitably begins to intrude on the exclusive domain of the *family*, going beyond Scripture and exerting authority that belongs to the *parents*, not to the *pastors*.

But the opposite can also occur. Sometimes a man decides he should be not only the *head* of his home, but also its *pastor* and *king*. He decides he *is* the elder board, and he *is* the government, and that he doesn't have to listen to *anyone*. That's a power grab that inevitably results in disaster for the family, for without the *spiritual* authority of the church and the *legal* authority of government, there is nothing to provide a check or balance to the father's power, and he becomes a little tyrant *ruling*—and inevitably *ruining*—his little kingdom. In such cases, it is the proper domain of the church to provide spiritual correction by means of church discipline. Moreover, if the man crosses the line into *criminal* neglect or abuse, he has then intruded into the government's right to protect the safety of its citizens, and it is appropriate for a body such as child protective services or the police to intervene.

It can transpire that both the church and the family can exceed their authority and intrude on the other exclusive domains. However, world history shows us that it is often *government* which exceeds its authority and intrudes on the exclusive domain of the church and family.

History is replete with tragic examples of tyrannical governments who ignore the divine limits on their authority and *trample* on the exclusive domain of the church or the family, and then *persecute* those who choose to obey God rather than them.

That is why American Christians should be so grateful, for we have been unusually blessed to have so much freedom for so long. As I mentioned in the introduction, for the church to have *this* much freedom from persecution for *this* long is an anomaly in church history. And because we've had *so* much freedom for *so* long, we've never really had to think very deeply about how to recognize if the government has begun to intrude on the spiritual authority of the church.

But now times are changing, and it seems increasingly likely that churches will face open hostility from local, state, or federal governments in the near future. In fact, in some contexts, open hostility has already begun.

Here are several suggestions for how to recognize when the government is exceeding its authority and intruding on the exclusive domain of the church. The government intrudes on the spiritual authority God delegated exclusively to the church in the following four scenarios:

Scenario 1

• • • • • • • • • •

The government attempts to limit or forbid the assembling of the saints for a lengthy, unreasonable, or indefinite period of time under the guise of "public health," a "state of emergency," or "national unity."

The Greek term for "church" is *ecclesia*, which means "an assembly." So assembling is definitional for the church. To gather together is a core, non-negotiable aspect of the church's identity and mission. A "church" which doesn't regularly assemble is, by definition, not a church. It may be a Bible conference, a Christian broadcast, a helpful website, a mission, or a ministry—but it is not a "church."

This is made clear by the Lord's instructions in Hebrews 10:25 and many other passages, which *command* believers to gather together *regularly* and *continuously.*

> Let us hold fast the confession of our hope without wavering, for He who promised is faithful; and let us consider how to stimulate one another to love and good deeds, not forsaking our own assembling together, as is the habit of some, but encouraging one another; and all the more as you see the day drawing near.
> (Hebrews 10:23–25)

The book of Acts tells us that believers gathered "on the Lord's day" (Sunday) and for several other times of fellowship during the week. They gathered regularly, habitually, and continuously. That is the Lord's *intent*, and that is the Lord's *command*.

"But wait a minute," someone might say. "Are you saying it is a sin to ever miss or cancel a Sunday service?"

The first reply to that question needs to be that yes, this text makes it clear that missing services or canceling them is a much more serious matter than contemporary believers apparently consider it to be. In our day, virtually *any reason* is considered acceptable for skipping services. It is clear that many, many believers no longer take this command seriously. The initial reply to such a question needs to be to reiterate the point of Hebrews 10:25 which is this: Don't forsake the assembling of yourselves together!

But while the point of the passage is that skipping services is sin, the Lord in His wisdom does include an appropriate measure of Christian freedom to believers in light of the grammar and wording of the text that describes this. The participle "forsaking" is in the present tense in Greek, indicating continual or ongoing action. Combined with the word "habit" which modifies it, it is clear that *temporary* cessation of the assembly is permitted by the Lord, whereas *continual or habitual* cessation from assembling is not permitted.

Therefore, for believers to miss a service on rare occasions in order to travel for work or a family event is not sin, but to do so regularly or habitually is sin. Similarly, for church leaders to cancel services for a few weeks because of a blizzard, a natural disaster, a national emergency, or a pandemic would not violate the command as long as the cancellation is *temporary*. But while there is a measure of applicational freedom granted in the grammar of the command of Hebrews 10:25, the force of the command should not be overlooked: The regular assembly of the local church is a high priority and is a binding command given to us by God.

It is important to underscore that the grammar and content of Hebrews 10:25 and other passages make it clear that *only temporary* and *reasonable* exceptions to the binding rule of regular assembly can be made. And it is also important to note that the authority and responsibility to determine what is "reasonable" and "temporary" belongs to the *elders* of the church, not to the state. *Only* the elders have the spiritual authority to cancel services, and even they can only do so on a *temporary* basis, because Hebrews 10:25 is a binding, divine command.

Elders can certainly take governmental input into account in making a decision to temporarily cancel services, but it is ultimately *their* decision to make, for *Christ, not Caesar, is the Head of the church.* The Lord delegated authority over His church to spiritual elders, not to state officials—to pastors, not to politicians.

Scenario 2
• • • • • • • • • •

The government intrudes on the spiritual authority God delegated exclusively to the church when it attempts to regulate or restrict the content of the church's teaching or the elements of the church's worship.

The government has no right to regulate the content of the church's teaching and preaching. For example, the state cannot tell the church to stop teaching that homosexuality is a sin, for it has no authority to contradict the Word of God or to silence the voices of His ambassadors. And just as representatives of the government cannot force the exclusion of doctrines which they don't like, they also cannot command the inclusion of ideologies which they do like.

Likewise, the government neither has the right to demand that extrabiblical elements be *included* in church worship services, nor that biblical elements be *excluded*. For example, the government cannot demand that churches include a political or patriotic symbol, element, or statement in the worship service (e.g., a flag, a pledge, or a national anthem). Nor can the government demand that churches exclude preaching, prayer, fellowship, worship, etc.

Therefore, in the context of the Covid-related controversies of 2020, churches who refused to omit singing from their worship services, despite being pressured to do so by several state governors, were correct to take a stand on that issue—for God's Holy Word *commands* worshippers to sing (e.g., Psalm 105:2, Ephesians 5:19–20).

Scenario 3
• • • • • • • • • •

The government intrudes on the spiritual authority God delegated exclusively to the church when it attempts to control or interfere in the church's process of choosing and ordaining spiritual leaders.

Historically, one of the ways that governments have attempted to exert unlawful and illegitimate control over the church is to meddle in the selection, training, ordination, or hiring of church leaders, staff, volunteers, or board members. Such attempts must be vigorously resisted by the true church, for it inevitably transfers the headship of the church from Christ to Caesar.

Scenario 4
• • • • • • • • • •

The government intrudes on the spiritual authority God delegated exclusively to the church when it attempts to stop or restrict the church from preaching the gospel to the lost.

The King of kings gave His church the Great Commission, and no lower authority can countermand HIS command. Therefore, the so-called "anti-proselytism" laws which many countries have adopted are not to be obeyed by Christians. As the apostle Paul put it, ". . . woe is me if I do not preach the gospel" (1 Corinthians 9:16). If evangelism ever becomes illegal in America, we can be as "wise as serpents" in how and when we share the gospel, but we must do our job as ambassadors of the King of kings, and accept that our obedience to the Lord may come at great personal cost. For whenever and wherever governments try to impede evangelism, believers must follow the example of the apostles by "obeying God rather than men." Forbidding believers from making disciples is a clear violation of a command God has given to the church, and therefore a red-light issue.

Summing Up

To sum up our key points, in this section we've seen that each of the three areas of authority has areas of EXCLUSIVE DOMAIN delegated by God, and that none of the three has the right to intrude upon the authority God has given exclusively to one of the other areas. When one attempts to do so, God intends the other two to RESIST and RESTRAIN that overreach. It was not America's founding fathers who first designed a system of checks and balances on human authority; God Himself had already done so!

THE GREEN-LIGHT PRINCIPLE

· · · · · · · · · · · · · · · · · · ·

Now, of course, not every issue is an issue of exclusive domain. There are also areas of *shared domain*.

Areas of shared domain occur when Scripture commands, instructs, authorizes, or requires something of more than one area of authority.

For example, both the church and the family are given the responsibility to teach the Word of God to the next generation. So the spiritual education of children is a responsibility shared by the church *and* by the family—but not by the state.

In areas of *shared authority*, the Lord intends the different spheres to cooperate and work together by voluntary and mutual consent.

"Voluntary and mutual consent" means that no area of authority should impose its will on another, or coerce, threaten, or manipulate the other in any way. But it also means that none of them should withdraw, isolate itself, and shut out the others. God's design was not for there to be three disconnected areas of competing authority, but rather that there should be three interconnected areas of cooperating authority.

Good relationships are key to the fulfillment of the Lord's design, so government officials, church leaders, and heads of households should work hard to establish and maintain close, cordial, respectful, and mutually beneficial relationships.

THE YELLOW-LIGHT PRINCIPLE

• • • • • • • • • • • • • • • • • • • •

It would be straightforward if there was always a clear and simple red-light or green-light answer to every question related to the proper domain of the three areas of authority. But the reality is that there are also yellow-light issues—areas of *disputable domain*.

As in driving on the road, for each area of authority there are red-light issues—in this analogy, matters where God has clearly said, as it were, "Stop! Don't enter that intersection, for it is the proper domain of another area!" Similarly, there are also green-light issues—matters where God has clearly said to all the areas of authority, "Go, but stay in your lane and be courteous to the other drivers."

But not every issue which arises between families, the church, and the government is clearly a red or a green issue. Some are yellow issues. These are disputable matters where judgment calls may have to be made—areas where the leaders of each area of authority need to make a loving, wise, and responsible decision based on multiple factors. In yellow-light issues, the leaders of local churches may reach different yet biblically valid conclusions about what is best for their own congregations. In such cases, they should respect each others' decisions.

When driving, a yellow light means a responsible driver has to make a decision whether it is *better* to hit the brakes or *better* to proceed. Note that the key word here is "*better.*" Some issues are not a right-or-wrong decision, but rather a better-or-worse decision. When there is a red light or a green light, there is no decision to make. It's simply a matter of obedience to the law. It is right to follow the law, and it is wrong to break it. But at a yellow light, the issue becomes not "right or wrong," but rather "better or worse." The driver needs to make a *judgment call* based on the circumstances at the time. And the best decision can depend on a variety of factors, such as how far away the intersection is, whether there is snow on the ground, whether pedestrians are present, and how close the person behind is following.

So a positive outcome in yellow-light issues depends on the *wisdom* of the leadership of each area. Wise governmental, ecclesiastical, and family leaders should be able to work out mutually acceptable solutions in these kind of situations. Doing so usually requires both a cordial tone and a willingness to defer to one another in order to reach a constructive and mutually agreeable resolution.

Historically, American church leaders have not needed to hone their negotiating skills, since the government rarely got even close to intruding on church authority. But the more the country tilts toward big-government policies, the more church elder boards will need to become savvy and strong negotiators.

Jesus told His disciples to be "as shrewd as serpents and innocent as doves" (Matthew 10:16). In yellow-light issues, it is important for believers to be shrewd—having a well-considered and smart strategy for defending and advancing the best interests of the church without needlessly offending governmental officials. But it is also vitally important to be as "innocent as doves"—never using evil means to accomplish righteous ends, and treating government officials with the kindness, respect, submission, and honor the Lord has commanded.

One of the best ways to learn how to be as shrewd as serpents and innocent as doves is to learn from church leaders in other countries. Unlike in America, churches in some other countries have had to operate under constant pressure from heavy-handed governments for decades—or even centuries. So they have a vast measure of experience in navigating legally and spiritually complex issues.

In the fifteen years I served as a missionary professor in the former Soviet Union, I had the privilege of observing Russian, Ukrainian, and Central Asian leaders applying the Matthew 10:16 principle to some very difficult and complex situations. Here are a few of the many lessons they can teach us:

Some Lessons

• • • • • • • • • •

LESSON 1
Green-light issues should be used to build positive relationships with local government and law enforcement.

If you don't work hard at building cordial, cooperative, mutually beneficial, and even friendly relationships with government officials on green-light issues, you will have a much harder time dealing with them when yellow-light issues arise—and you won't have the allies you need in government when you face red-light intrusions. So spend the time and effort necessary to establish and maintain cordial and friendly personal relationships with local authorities.

For example, on national holidays, Ukrainian pastors would personally deliver beautiful nature calendars with Bible verses on them, homemade desserts, or other non-monetary gifts to their local city hall and police headquarters. Several times throughout the year, they would drop by for a five-minute courtesy visit just to ask if they have any personal prayer requests. They would put forth a lot of effort to make friends with local government and law enforcement, and those cordial relationships served to greatly protect their churches, and to prevent enemies of the gospel from shutting down evangelistic outreaches, church construction projects, etc.

It is vitally important to apply the wisdom Jesus taught in Luke 16:

> And his master praised the unrighteous manager because he had acted shrewdly; for the sons of this age are more shrewd in relation to their own kind than the sons of light.

And I say to you, make friends for yourselves by means of the wealth of unrighteousness, so that when it fails, they will receive you into the eternal dwellings.

(Luke 16:8–9)

LESSON 2
If a yellow-light situation has turned adversarial, be sure to take early and decisive initiative to reach a solution which limits the consequences of the dispute and the damage to your relationship with the government.

It can be tempting to confuse courage with stubbornness, so on yellow-light issues, make sure you're not making a bad situation worse.

Leaders in post-Soviet countries can be an enigma to Western observers. On the one hand, they demonstrated unbreakable resolve and remarkable courage during seventy years of Communist persecution. But on the other hand, they can seem surprisingly quick to cave in and seek a compromise which will pacify hostile government officials when confronted with yellow-light issues. Since never backing down is considered to be evidence of personal courage in American pop culture, we wonder how these heroes of the faith can have a backbone of steel in red-light situations, and then back down so quickly in yellow-light ones. What we don't realize is that the never-back-down attitude of our culture may be a vice, not a virtue. We can learn from post-Soviet leaders that choosing your battles wisely means you are shrewd, not weak.

So keep in mind and apply the wisdom Jesus gave in Matthew 5:25–26:

Make friends quickly with your opponent at law while you are with him on the way, so that your opponent may not hand you over to the judge, and the judge to the officer, and you be thrown into prison. Truly I say to you, you will not come out of there until you have paid up the last cent.

(Matthew 5:25–26)

Lesson 3

If you don't have an unbreakable resolve to stand firm on red-light issues no matter the cost, you'll get run over on yellow-light issues as well.

Hostile officials should have no doubt in their minds that you will "obey God rather than men" if they force an issue where a biblical command is at stake.

Governments throughout the former Soviet Union know that believers are willing to pay an incredible personal cost to obey Christ. They remember the Soviet era, when pastors endured prisons and gulags, martyrs gave their lives, and churches could not be stamped out or stopped despite intense persecution. Knowing that churches won't cave in on red-light issues is a wonderful restraining influence, for who wants to start a fight that seventy years of history proved even the might of the Soviet Union couldn't win?

So remember to heed the exhortations of 1 Corinthians 15:58 and 16:13–14:

> Therefore, my beloved brethren, be steadfast, immovable, always abounding in the work of the Lord, knowing that your toil is not in vain in the Lord.
> (1 Corinthians 15:58)

> Be on the alert, stand firm in the faith, act like men, be strong. Let all that you do be done in love.
> (1 Corinthians 16:13–14)

Please recognize that yellow-light issues between churches and the government can be particularly difficult to navigate. The crucial ingredient for success is *wisdom*. Be sure to pray for it (James 1:5), diligently study the Scriptures to obtain it (Psalm 119:105), and import it in the form of good advice from a multitude of counselors (Proverbs 11:14, 15:22, 24:6). Issues of *disputable domain* are often complex, so as in all of life, we must humble ourselves and diligently seek the Lord's will and the Lord's wisdom.

Do not let kindness and truth leave you;
Bind them around your neck,
Write them on the tablet of your heart.
So you will find favor and good repute
In the sight of God and man.
Trust in the LORD with all your heart
And do not lean on your own understanding.
In all your ways acknowledge Him,
And He will make your paths straight.
Do not be wise in your own eyes;
Fear the LORD and turn away from evil.
(Proverbs 3:3–7)

5

Summary

In this book, so far we have considered three important and practical questions:

QUESTION 1
What should a believer's attitude and perspective be toward human government?

QUESTION 2
How can we know when we are supposed to submit to government (Romans 13:1), and when we must "obey God rather than men" (Acts 5:29)?

QUESTION 3
How can we know when the government has exceeded the limits of its divinely ordained authority and intruded on authority which God has given exclusively to the church or to the family?

We answered question #1 by considering seven ways we should view government from Romans 12:14–13:7:

We should view government officials as:

1. individuals with eternal souls;
2. having authority delegated from God;
3. having a responsibility to restrain evil and protect good;
4. a minister of God's wrath against evil;
5. a safeguard for when the human conscience fails;
6. servants of God, not masters of men;
7. deserving of appropriate respect and honor.

We answered question #2 by studying five key verses and deriving from them five key principles of a Biblical Theology of Government:

1. Since only God has unlimited authority, all delegated authority is limited authority.
2. Governments exceed their delegated authority when they either require disobedience against God, or restrict obedience to God.

3. Governments exceed their authority when they demand worship or prevent worship.

4. Governments exceed their delegated authority when they intrude on authority God has delegated exclusively to the church or the family.

5. When governments exceed their delegated authority, believers have both the right and the duty to obey God rather than men.

We answered question #3 by discussing the three primary areas of authority which God has ordained, and proposing a traffic-light paradigm for evaluating the extent, limits, and overlapping authority of the family, the church, and the government:

CONSIDERATION 1
"Red Light" issues occur when one sphere of authority attempts to intrude on the authority which God has exclusively delegated to another sphere of authority. In such cases, we must take a strong and uncompromising stand against the intrusion in order to preserve the divinely mandated order. The government intrudes on the authority God delegated exclusively to the church in the following instances:

1. When it attempts to limit or forbid the assembling of the saints for a lengthy, unreasonable, or indefinite period of time under the guise of "public health," a "state of emergency," or "national unity";

2. When it attempts to regulate or restrict the content of the church's teaching or the elements of its worship;

3. When it attempts to control or interfere in the church's process of choosing and ordaining spiritual leaders;

4. When it attempts to stop or restrict the church from preaching the gospel to the lost.

CONSIDERATION 2
"Green Light" issues are those in which two or three areas of authority have overlapping authority, because God has delegated a task or responsibility to more than one area. In such cases,

we should cooperate and work together with other areas of authority, for God intends the three areas to be interconnected and synergistic.

In areas of *shared authority*, the Lord intends the different spheres to cooperate and work together by voluntary and mutual consent.

CONSIDERATION 3

Yellow-Light issues are disputable and complex matters in which deciding whether to resist or cooperate with another area of authority is a difficult decision. In such cases, we need to pray for wisdom (James 1:5), diligently study the Scriptures (Psalm 119:105), and seek good advice from a multitude of counselors (Proverbs 11:14, 15:22, 24:6).

Jesus taught us to ". . . be as shrewd as serpents and innocent as doves" (Matthew 10:16). In yellow-light issues, we need to be shrewd—having a well-considered and smart strategy for defending and advancing the best interests of the church. But we also need to be as "innocent as doves"—never using evil means to accomplish righteous ends, and we should treat government officials with the kindness, respect, submission, and honor the Lord has commanded.

6

Conclusion and Application

Throughout this book, we've tried to follow the steps of the "theological pyramid" so that our conclusions will be based on the Word of God, and not on personal, cultural, or political biases.

So we'll conclude with a few suggestions for the fourth step: practical application.

POINT OF APPLICATION 1:
Proclaim the gospel of Christ!

It is heartbreaking to observe the often pitiable state of the American family, government, and church. All three jurisdictions are in serious need of spiritual revival and reformation! Since the functionality or dysfunctionality of each jurisdiction results from the cumulative effect of the righteousness or unrighteousness of its members, the key to reforming each jurisdiction is the spiritual transformation of its members. We must always remember that:

- Jurisdictional reformation requires spiritual transformation.
- Spiritual transformation comes only through the new birth.
- Therefore, only the gospel of Jesus Christ can effect true reformation.

Scripture teaches us to give Jesus "first place in everything" (Col. 1:18). It reminds us that the gospel of Christ's death for sin, His burial, and His resurrection are "of first importance" (1 Cor. 15:3). And it commands us to proclaim the good news, "that if you confess with your mouth Jesus as Lord, and believe in your heart that God raised Him from the dead, you will be saved" (Rom. 10:9).

So our first and most important point of application needs to be a renewed commitment to the centrality of the gospel and the fulfillment of the Great Commission:

All authority has been given to Me in heaven and on earth. Go therefore and make disciples of all the nations, baptizing them in the name of the Father and the Son and the Holy Spirit, teaching them to observe all that I commanded you; and lo, I am with you always, even to the end of the age. (Matthew 28:18-20)

POINT OF APPLICATION 2
Choose leaders prayerfully, carefully, and wisely.

IN THE FAMILY AREA: If you are a young person, choose your spouse carefully. Your spouse *will* have authority over your future children. For *their* sake, choose wisely! Make sure the criteria by which you are evaluating a potential spouse is biblical, intentional, and substantive. Superficial, frivolous, and immature criteria which fails to prioritize godly character will lead to disaster and heartache down the road. "Like a gold ring in a pig's snout is a beautiful woman who lacks discretion" (Proverbs 11:22). "Man looks on the outward appearance, but the LORD looks at the heart" (1 Samuel 16:7).

IN THE CHURCH AREA: Churches need to take the selection, evaluation, and affirmation of pastors, elders, and deacons extremely seriously, for whoever they ordain will have spiritual authority and sacred responsibilities (Hebrews 13:17). Especially in situations where churches must navigate red-light or yellow-light issues of church/state authority, it is vital that church leaders be men who meet the biblical qualifications for elders and deacons (1 Timothy 3, Titus 1), and that they be men of "good reputation, full of the Spirit and of wisdom" (Acts 6:3).

IN THE GOVERNMENT AREA: Endeavor to be a model citizen, one who honors, respects, and submits to the authorities God sovereignly places over you (Romans 13:1,7). Be diligent to pray for your local, state, and federal officials so that you may "lead a tranquil and quiet life in all godliness and dignity" (1 Timothy 2:1–4). Be sure to remember that human governments are made up of human beings who are created in the image of God, and have an eternal soul. Be a good ambassador of the gospel of Jesus Christ to them, and to all your fellow citizens (Titus 3:1–8)!

POINT OF APPLICATION 3
The time to develop a robust and practical biblical theology of the proper roles and responsibilities of government, the church, and the family is now—not when you're in a yellow-light or red-light crisis between the three areas of authority.

IN THE FAMILY AREA: Husbands and wives should study together what Scripture says about this topic so that they may be unified in their convictions before they face difficult decisions. If the government makes spanking of their children illegal, is that a red-, yellow-, or green-light issue? If either the government or the church tries to compel families toward either public schooling or home schooling, is that a red-, yellow-, or green-light issue?

IN THE CHURCH AREA: Church leadership teams should study what Scripture says about this topic together so that they may be unified in their convictions before they face difficult decisions. How will you determine if governmental public safety regulations, requirements, or restrictions are red-, yellow-, or green-light issues? How will you respond to anti-discrimination laws if they either limit what can be taught about sin, or compel the use of politically correct language (such as gender-neutral pronouns)? How will you avoid the extremes of either exerting legalistic control over families or failing to hold them to biblical standards of holiness?

IN THE GOVERNMENT AREA: Believers who hold positions of authority and responsibility in government should study what Scripture says about this topic before they face difficult decisions between following orders and following Christ. How will you determine when you should "do your job" and when you should "take a stand"? What tasks or orders are green-light issues where you will joyfully and energetically contribute to the goals of your superiors? What tasks or orders are yellow-light issues where you need to respectfully and wisely use your influence to try to modify an ill-advised decision? What tasks or orders are red-light issues where you must "obey God rather than men"?

Point of Application 4
Count the cost and resolve to follow Christ, no matter the cost!

As I stated at the beginning, the fact that American Christians have experienced almost no persecution for so many generations is a highly unusual historical fact. For most believers in most countries throughout most of church history, persecution has been either a periodic or a constant reality.

If harder times lie ahead for believers in America, will you stand or fall, hold fast or fold? Will you be a faithful ambassador of the gospel regardless of whether the future is filled with peace or persecution? Will you speak the truth in love even if you are reviled and oppressed? Will you follow Christ no matter the cost?

My prayer is that—come what may—you will glorify Christ by faithfully serving Him with humility, love, and courage. May the Lord bless and keep you! May you be found faithful at His glorious appearing! And may He grant you great encouragement through the marvelous promises He revealed through the apostle Peter:

> Blessed be the God and Father of our Lord Jesus Christ, who according to His great mercy has caused us to be born again to a living hope through the resurrection of Jesus Christ from the dead, to obtain an inheritance which is imperishable and undefiled and will not fade away, reserved in heaven for you, who are protected by the power of God through faith for a salvation ready to be revealed in the last time. In this you greatly rejoice, even though now for a little while, if necessary, you have been distressed by various trials, so that the proof of your faith, being more precious than gold which

is perishable, even though tested by fire, may be found to result in praise and glory and honor at the revelation of Jesus Christ; and though you have not seen Him, you love Him, and though you do not see Him now, but believe in Him, you greatly rejoice with joy inexpressible and full of glory, obtaining as the outcome of your faith the salvation of your souls.

(1 Peter 1:3–9)

Soli Deo Gloria

Appendix 1

The "Separation of Church and State"

American democracy was founded on the core principle which we have been discussing in this book: that the family, the government, and the church have their own jurisdictions of authority. As we have seen, the relationship between the three spheres is designed to be overlapping and symbiotic:

- Churches influence families and the government through the preaching of God's Word;
- Families influence the church and the state as active members and voting citizens;
- Government influences both churches and families by upholding the rule of law without favoritism.

The "circles" should overlap in mutually beneficial ways, but they are, nonetheless, separate jurisdictions.

America's founding fathers sought to apply this biblical principle through a legal concept popularly known as "the separation of church and state." Originally, this was an affirmation by the founding fathers of the biblical truth that God has delegated a separate jurisdiction of sovereign authority to the church, and that the government must submit to God by recognizing and respecting each church's sovereignty over its own faith and practice.

This is why, from a legal point of view, churches have rightly been treated in American law much like embassies—as diplomatic outposts of the Kingdom of God in the kingdoms of men. For example, churches are exempt from taxes for the same reason foreign embassies are—because the authority to tax presupposes and asserts jurisdictional sovereignty over the entity being taxed. Since Christ, not Caesar, is sovereign over the church, churches as legal entities have been considered tax exempt. So have children, because their parents are their legal guardians. But moms and dads, church members and clergy, are all expected to pay taxes as individuals, for they are citizens of the state and therefore under its jurisdiction.

These traditional aspects of the American legal system seem

to have been derived from biblical teaching. In Matthew 17:24-27 and 22:21, Jesus presupposes that the state has the authority to tax its citizens, and teaches that individual Christians should pay their taxes. But He also makes an important distinction in Matthew 17:26 when He says, "the sons are exempt." The plural of "sons" has been traditionally understood as a reference to the church as a corporate and spiritual body. The church in its corporate sense, Jesus says, "is exempt" because it is under the jurisdiction of God, not the state. So the American system which taxes individual believers, but gives tax-exempt status to churches, corresponds well to biblical teaching. Perhaps this is one reason why God has so abundantly blessed the United States financially.

But the underlying concept is certainly not unique to the American context. Throughout the world, countries recognize that foreign embassies are under the sovereign authority of their own governments, not the government of the country where the embassy is located. But what they don't always recognize is that no earthly government has sovereignty over the church—only Christ does. Believers are His ambassadors, and churches are His embassies.

Therefore, the church and the state are "separate, but equal" in their respective jurisdictions. If that principle is abandoned, it will inevitably lead to either the domination of the church by the state, or *vice versa*. And both state churches and churchless states will easily and inevitably crush the rights and liberties of both secular and religious families, because the combined powers of two jurisdictions merged into one would be overwhelming.

So the concept of "the separation of church and state" is not only biblically sound but is also vitally important to liberty, and has been core to the success of the United States and other democracies.

But sadly, anti-Christian political forces are seeking to twist that principle into something never intended by the founding fathers of the USA. Under the banner of the "separation of church and state," they are trying to push churches out of the public arena altogether.

To use our visual illustration, they think the "circles" of church and state should not overlap *at all*—in fact they shouldn't even *touch*. And it is becoming increasingly clear that more and more of these anti-Christian political forces don't think the church's sphere of sovereign jurisdiction should even be allowed to exist.

Calls for the tax-exempt status of churches and religious institutions to be revoked are much more sinister than just an effort to hurt them financially. It is an attempt to strike a fatal blow against a foundational principle of democracy by asserting the sovereignty of the state over the church. Again, to tax an entity, the government must have sovereignty over that entity. And for the government to assert this kind of sovereignty over the church is no small matter. As Supreme Court Justice John Marshall famously pointed out in 1819, "The power to tax is the power to destroy."

The enemies of the cross regularly cite "the separation of church and state" to justify their efforts to push churches out of the public arena and prevent them from having any influence in society at all. But at the same time, they have no problem calling for the state to intrude into matters of the church. They are actively pushing for legislation that would *gag* churches and *compel* them to accept secular views of gender, sexuality, and marriage. They are attempting to use the power of government to impose their will on the church.

In other words, what they want is not a "wall of separation" between the jurisdictions of the church and the state, but rather a "one-way gate." This is hypocrisy, and it should be vigorously opposed. If they are successful, the one-way gate they seek to build will not only limit the influence of churches, but it will open the door to tyranny.

Appendix 2

The Individual as
the Fourth Sphere
of Divinely-Delegated Authority

The focus of this study has been on relating the distinct but complementary jurisdictions of three external spheres of authority which God has ordained to bring order and blessing to human societies. It has particularly focused on the proper role of government in relation to the church. So it is beyond the scope of this book to adequately address the relationship between the individual and the three societal jurisdictions.

However, it is important to at least note here that when God created Adam and Eve, He delegated authority to them to "rule over" the earth and to "to subdue it" (Genesis 1:26-28). Therefore, the individual can be considered a fourth jurisdiction of divinely delegated authority.

As the creation mandate is traced throughout Scripture, it becomes clear that God has given each individual a unique sphere of personal freedom and responsibility. But the authority which God delegated to the individual is, like all delegated authority, limited by God's commandments. In Scripture, individuals are commanded to love God and others above self, to submit to the properly exercised authority of three societal jurisdictions, and to live in a manner consistent with the character and purposes of God. By God's command, the fourth jurisdiction is one which must be governed by the law of *love*, by *humility*, by *holiness*, and by Spirit-filled *self-control* (Galatians 5:23, 1 Corinthians 9:27, 1 Timothy 4:11-16).

While I must leave it to other authors (from the past and in the future) to more thoroughly address this vital topic, I'd like to briefly suggest a core biblical concept for understanding the extent and limits of individual authority:

Both the dignity and the responsibilities of the individual are rooted in the fact that each person bears the image of God (e.g., Genesis 1:27), has inalienable rights which were given to him by God (e.g., Psalm 8), must obey the commands of

God (e.g., Matthew 22:37-40), and is accountable to God for how he uses or misuses the abilities he possesses because he is made in the image of God (e.g., 2 Corinthians 5:10).

The Relationship Between the Image of God and Individual Dignity:

Though the image of God has been marred and distorted by sin, each individual is still a divine image bearer. Therefore, any unjust action which degrades, humiliates, violates, harms, wounds, or murders an individual is a sin against God. This is a key reason why tyrannical governments sin against God when they implement or allow abortion, forced sterilization, euthanasia, and other violations of human rights. It is why no one has the authority to kill an unborn child. It is why all forms of sexual coercion and abuse are sinful and evil. It is why no man has the right to degrade or humiliate his wife and children in the name of "submission." It is why legalistic church leaders abuse their spiritual authority when they "go beyond what is written" (1 Corinthians 4:6) and intrude into the proper domain of the family or the individual. Since human beings are made in God's image, no external authority has the right to violate basic human rights, and all who do so will be judged by God.

The Relationship Between the Image of God and Individual Responsibility:

Being made in the image of God also brings responsibility. We dishonor God when we fail to reflect His glory in the use of our gifts and abilities. This is why each individual is held accountable by God for the stewardship of his body, time, talents, and possessions. It is why all of life is sacred. It is why even seemingly mundane things like personal hygiene are not only matters of health, but also of worship. It is why a good work ethic is not just an economic necessity, but a spiritual obligation. It is why education, the arts, science, and sports have spiritual significance. All of these things (and more) are rooted in the gifts and abilities which mankind—and mankind alone—possesses because individuals are made in the image of God. Since we are invested with such dignity, we have corresponding responsibility.

In Summary

Since each individual is made in God's image, those who have responsibility in the three external jurisdictions in which God has delegated authority must be careful not to transgress the boundaries of the individual dignity of other people.

Likewise, the individual must be careful not to misuse his gifts and abilities in order to sinfully rebel against the external authorities God has established.

TMAI's mission is aligned with our Lord's great commission in Matthew 28:19-20 to make disciples of all nations. We believe that the most strategic way to do this is to train gifted and qualified indigenous church leaders, giving them the tools they need to plant and pastor Bible-centered, Christ-exalting churches.

At TMAI, our core values are based on biblical principles, and shape everything we do:

AUTHORITY OF SCRIPTURE
The inerrant and sufficient Word of God is our ultimate authority. Therefore, we submit to His Word in all areas of life and ministry (2 Tim. 3:16).

CENTRALITY OF THE LOCAL CHURCH
The church is the pillar and support of the truth (1 Tim. 3:15), the institution that Christ promised to build (Matt. 16:18). Therefore, our training has as its goal the strengthening of His church.

PRIORITY OF THE GOSPEL
The gospel of Jesus Christ alone is the power of God unto salvation to everyone who believes (Rom. 1:16). Therefore, fundamental to our theological education is an accurate and thorough proclamation of this true gospel.

IMPORTANCE OF INTEGRITY
We uphold God's high standard of holiness and integrity for spiritual leaders (1 Tim. 3). Therefore, we provide accountability in doctrinal, financial, and academic matters.

VALUE OF RESPECT
We approach international ministry with a commitment to honoring our co-laborers in other countries. Therefore, we purpose from the outset to train in a way so as to entrust the training ministries into their capable hands (2 Tim. 2:2).

About Shepherd Press Publications

They are gospel driven.
They are heart focused.
They are life changing.

Our Invitation to You

We passionately believe that what we are publishing can be of benefit to you, your family, your friends, and your work colleagues. So we are inviting you to join our online mailing list so that we may reach out to you with news about our latest and forthcoming publications, and with special offers.

Visit:

www.shepherdpress.com/newsletter

and provide your name and email address.

Why America Hates Biblical Christianity
David A. Harrell
Paperback, 214 pages
ISBN 9781633422377

As never before in American history, Christians are witnessing biblical values being replaced by laws that impose a godless, immoral, oppressive social agenda on their country. The overall disdain political and religious liberal activists have toward conservative values in general and authentic Christianity in particular has produced an ideological civil war that is raging out of control. But many people sense there's something more sinister going on, something beyond the realm of ideological divides, something evil, perhaps even eschatological—and that's the position of this book.

"Dave Harrell skillfully shows from Scripture how true followers of Christ should respond—and why we must remain steadfast—even as the moral fabric of American society is unraveling all around us."
—John MacArthur

". . . clear, insightful, encouraging analysis of our culture's spiritual meltdown, and our duty as Christians to respond with courage and conviction. I'm certain you will be emboldened and uplifted by this excellent book."
—Phil Johnson

The Quest for Truth
Shannon Hurley
Large Paperback, 248 pages
ISBN 9781633421820

This is more than just a book; it is a road map. It is penned with passion, concern, and thoughtful consideration for its readers. It provides guidance through the wonderful teaching of God's Word, the Bible, in a systematic and comprehensive way. It does not assume that its readers have a lot of knowledge, and it cuts a careful course through key Old Testament and New Testament aspects of the gospel of the Lord Jesus Christ. Readers working their way through this—whether as individuals or in a group—will complete the fifteen chapters with a robust and comprehensive understanding of God-centered Christianity.

"*The Quest for Truth* is a helpful primer to Christian thought, designed to facilitate evangelism and discipleship through interactive lessons."
—John MacArthur

"You will find this work to be Scripture-based, God-exalting, and Christ-centered. Whether you are a new believer, a mature Christian, or one who is considering the claims of Jesus Christ, I want to urge you to dig into, devour, and digest every page of this critically important book."
—Steven J. Lawson